Selected Poems of Kim Namjo

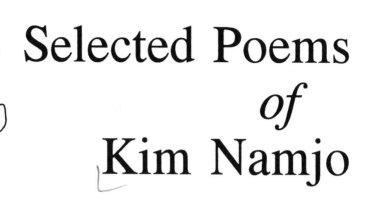

Selected Poems
of
Kim Namjo

Translated by
David R. McCann
Hyunjae Yee Sallee

With an Afterword by
Kim Yunsik

East Asia Program
Cornell University
Ithaca, New York 14853

The Cornell East Asia Series publishes manuscripts on a wide variety of scholarly topics pertaining to East Asia. Manuscripts are published on the basis of camera-ready copy provided by the volume author or editor.

Inquiries should be addressed to Editorial Board, Cornell East Asia Series, East Asia Program, Cornell University, 140 Uris Hall, Ithaca, New York 14853.

Publication of *Selected Poems of Kim Namjo* was supported by a generous grant from the Korean Culture and Arts Foundation.

ISSN 1050-2955
ISBN 0-939657-05-8 cloth
ISBN 0-939657-63-5 paper

Contents

Contents

Contents

Contents

Page numbers following the poems refer to Kim Namjo's *Complete Poems* (CP), *Kim Namjo sijŏnjip*, Seoul, Somundang, 1986 or to her more recent *Christening of the Wind* (CW), *Param serye*, Seoul, Munhak segyesa, 1988. Poems in the final section, New Poems, were unpublished in 1993.

From *Life* (1953)

Flower

I am your fertile ground.
The seeds you carelessly scattered have now
burst into lovely flowers.
Now just come here, embrace these flowers of yours.
When you kiss me, I become
a shy flower, red as the bride's rouged cheek.

(CP 34)

Love

Illness like something long forgotten.
Ache I could not name, there by the northern
window as the days,
weary as the gulls' wings
soaked in the evening sea,
grew like scales.
One morning as I watched a flock of geese lift
and wing across the sky,
even as I started to weep
without ceasing,
suddenly, as if struck by an arrow,
I had come to know the name of my illness.

(CP 37)

From *Trees and Wind* (1958)

For Baby

1

Sunlight alights and plays by my baby's sleeping head.
Sunlight is the baby's guest.

Each day since baby was born
has been smooth as silk.
My child
who cannot see yet.

My baby sleeps sound all day long;
sleep is baby's cradle.
Held in sleep, my baby is growing.

Baby is a small garden of peace
a bubbling stream of joy.

Baby is a lamp for mother.
When I am with baby
my heart is clear and bright.

2

My baby has no name yet.
Like the charming new-born chick or puppy
that has no name,
my baby has no name yet.

Dawn or night,
or hazy evening

I have been searching and searching
among the numberless letters,
but there is no word so sweet
to call my baby.

The field of stars in the sky,
the pearls that lie piled beneath the sea:
Where can I find
a name for my baby?

My baby has no name yet.
As no one knows the name for the white flower
and the blue bird sent for the first time
from some far distant land,
I do not know the name yet
for my child.

(CP 123)

Evening Primrose

Neither for stars nor moon
did this flowering tree yearn.

Even this moonless night
the tree filled with blossoms
is waiting
just for darkness.

While sea gull cleans its feathers
in the cold waves
of the night sea,
the flower
glows in the darkness
with a light like the lamps
in a distant mountain village.

Darkness,
generous oil:
This flower knows
the sweet rest that follows
in peace and tranquility.

The passing wind
kisses the flower,
and as the night deepens
the flower becomes
even more graceful.

Weary at morning light,
like a butterfly, it folds its wings.

(CP 133)

Poem for June

The wind blowing
across the ripening barley field
makes waves that seem to be smiling,
while the grateful sunrays spill down their calming oil.

Breathing a deep breath of peace,
the spacious, cobalt sky
becomes a cleansing rain,
cascading into my heart.

The fields of ripening barley
become a village of selfless love
as the wind passes over them, smiling.

The barley fields call to mind
the billowing sea with its small and giant waves.
The field also recalls
the river with its waves of gold and silver.

By these green fields of growing barley,
let us write a poem of June, the wind, and the fresh
grain;
let us make a song, clear and green.

(CP 136)

From *A Flag of Sentiments* (1960)

A Flag of Sentiments

My heart is a flag
that has been hung unnoticed
in the void.

When fever and confusion overwhelm me,
I walk out to the snowy crossroads.
There the soothing shadow
covers the snowy path like smoke.
Does my heart's flag
listen to the music of snow?

If I had a wish,
I would have each sun set without regrets,
piling up silently as flower petals.
Is there no friend
whose heart is pure as the reach of white sands
where sorrow piercing as the king's note of surrender
has subsided?

My heart
is a flag.

In the unseen void
it sometimes weeps
and sometimes offers up a prayer.

(CP 151)

Migratory Bird

What am I going to call you?
What are you going to call me?
With no fond name to call each other
you and I, who met for a moment,
are standing before a long separation.

Like long shadows cast against the twilight glow
down the empty furrows of a harvested field,
I have been thinking of you all alone
in this season of the year.

Despite enduring the many kinds of trouble in life,
I have always dreaded parting from you.
Pining heart that yearns for you so blindly —
the sin of ardor
that has no Divine help —
this searing heart!

What am I going to call you?
What are you going to call me?

Some day after we have grown older together,
I might call you a sorrowful migratory bird
who cried for a short while by the window one day.

Once upon a time,
a certain person, like this one, lived;
and a certain heart, filled with longing, also lived.

Might it become a tale, one that has no guilt!

You and I now
are standing before a long separation.

(CP 154)

Child and Mother Napping

Daytime, eyes drooping,
for a moment mother
holding her child's hand as both sleep:

The child's face,
smooth as the round moon in the water;
eyes half-closed, half
open, gleaming faintly.

Like flowers bunched in clusters
or a basket full of well-ripened fruit,
the constant scent of flesh,
baby's smell.

Crossing the edge of dreams,
baby's mind and mother's;
call it an echo riding a golden cart,
or the spring winds
gently kissing:

As baby wakens
mother too opens her eyes;
when baby laughs, all at once
mother's heart is a sunrise.

Outside the papered door
whoever might come or go,
this place by baby's side
is mother's paradise.

(CP 165)

Farewell

A fallen leaf, autumn's flag;
as it waves, signals the separation.

Goodbye,
at your departure,
I too wave my small hand.

Autumn
is the season of departure,
concealing a passionate heart;
autumn is the season to endure the pain of parting
before a milestone, standing abandoned.
It is the season for
sending off my beloved,
for loving him so.

A soul at peace
is a blessed lantern lit by God;
I pray that you
may be given such light.

How I wish to give everything away in love.
How I wish to spend my life serving you.
Can you understand such a heart as mine?

Parting is giving also —
giving even more out of sadness.
Can you understand this heart of mine?

Waving my small hand,
should I smile
like the petal of a white flower?

I'd believe then—
love is alive in my heart,
no matter how far away.

(CP 167)

Moonlit Night

When I open the door a bit,
you peek in with such hesitation;
when I open it a little wider,
you gaze inside for a good while
with your gray, counter-beam light.

When I leave both doors flung open,
you do not enter;
instead, you sit high in the middle of the sky,
veiling the world with your silk gown.

A certain person long ago
did just as you have . . .
He never paid me a visit,
but unrolled for me a roll of silk instead.

(CP 188)

From *Music of the Pine Woods* (1963)

Flowing with the River

A cloud
is a rose
blooming at the heart of the sky.

As long as
I am flowing with the river current,
how could I not take you along,
my beloved, like a cloud in my arms?

With the charm of
a gallant gambler
a cloud, a white wooden boat,
yielding up all the meaning of life,
floats along without regret.

When I wash my black hair in the cool water
and then comb it,
an autumn tree's melody from an unknown place
fills the air.

Dreams become reality.
A mysterious fountain overflows nearby.

When I was younger
merely listening to the words of love made me dizzy;
now I greet each daybreak with a smile
and offer a silent prayer every night.

In this gliding boat, I am content
with you as my one lighted yellow lantern.

As long as
I flow with the river current
having ample room for you,
like the wind,
like lamplight, my beloved,
how could I not bring you along?

(CP 219)

Serenade

To the sky
to the limitless sky
just one voice
is calling you.

Considering
the raindrops
the sunlight
as gifts,
each and every day, I who am in love
live my life, offering my warm hands.

Tears and truth
I had never experienced before:
Because of you, how precious this anxiety
to me, the one in love.

To the sea, to the bottom of the deep sea
only one voice
is calling you.

Regarding an empty seat,
loneliness
as a gift,
I who am in love
live my life, comforting my heart
by touching it with a soothing hand.

Your body and soul are gleaming
with the most amazing light
I have ever witnessed;
I would plant my heart dying to see you,
in the earth of the world to come,
and I would pray
that we become as a deep-rooted tree.

To the end of the earth
only one voice
is calling you, my beloved.

(CP 220)

Beloved

1

Half of my beloved's spoken words
is his clear laughter;
half of his laughter
was like God's.
If I had not known my beloved,
I might not have noticed the sky at all.

2

Longing
is the disease
that dyes my whole body.
Since the lightning flashed that one time,
I have been leaning my head
against the great heart
with all my being.

3

The first season I knew my beloved
came from song,
and I constantly was writing poems to meet him.
The next season came from prayers,
and I always intend
to wash my hands
in expectation of our meeting.

Yesterday and today
the words sleep.

My eyes, though,
and my ears are
filled with the light.

(CP 222)

For You, My Beloved

My evening prayer
is long,
repeating just the one phrase.

Quietly opening my eyes
becomes a supplication
almost past belief.

Your soul
is filled with new-born light
to its inner core.

Even lying down alone
with my black hair loosened,
there has never been
so generous a love.

It is for you
that I live.
However precious, I would give you
anything.
Forgetting
what I gave before,
thinking only of the love
I have not wholly given,
my beloved.

Seeing you as if seeing the ring
around the moon

through falling snow.

Only for you
all things have a name,
and have gladness,
my love.

(CP 224)

First Snow

Snow is falling
white butterflies
that make the hands ache with cold.

Audible as a shout,
the sudden music
of this enchanted shower.

Snow is falling.
The magic of the sky
changing its garments.

> I would see the fire,
> your soul;
> I would see the tears,
> your soul.

This tired glory that will not live
even briefly without loving;
this tireless enchantment.

Snow is falling.
Butterflies
that have soaked in the light
to their heart's content.

(CP 242)

From *Winter Sea* (1967)

Music

In music, such a dangerous sea, I drowned.
Lost in consuming rapture, I wept.

The boundless clouds of my own sky
remain sorrowful
during my life's journey.
Though I wrote numerous poems,
not a single phrase saved me.

A person
spends half a life in vague confusion
and half
in the habit of easily being hurt.

I wish to remain
like trees in harmony
in the snowy woods,
like a peaceful evening
after a graceful sunset.

I am afraid of truth
and feel shame at lies.

For music, its exhausting ecstasy, I wept;
I wept for its wordless truth.

(CP 260)

The Winter Sea

I went out to the winter sea,
but the birds of unknown species,
those I longed to see, had died and were gone.

I tried to think of you,
but in the biting sea wind
the truth itself turned to tears
and froze.

The flames of
emptiness
set fire to furrows on the water.

Time
as always
is what teaches me.
I stood by the winter sea,
nodding.

The days remaining
may be few,

but I wish for the soul
in which the door
to the even more heated prayer
is opened after my prayer.

The days remaining
may be few,

but I have gone to the winter sea,
I have seen where the waters of bitter endurance
form the pillar of the ocean's deep.

(CP 261)

Late Snow

Ardor for music and
love for my baby sustain me.

A late, cold snow
falls in white and blue.

What an empty delirium
to write poetry,
to love,
even to have a religion!

For every moment of empty glory,
always
I live in sorrow, tears wetting my eyelids.
If truth is all that lasts forever,
then surely this sense of solitude
is eternal for a man.

The candle in the misty night
gleams against the late snow,
the flame tells me:
There is no turning back;
no matter what, there is no turning back.

And so, one ought to have lived well
from the very start.

The night, the music,
the snowflakes.

(CP 262)

Summer Days

Day after day
bird who flies off on delicate wings
and returns;

through the rain
through lightning
you dashed away like a shot
and today fold your wings.

On the long and weary
hot summer day
a child sleeps, brow cooled
by a fan.

Nothing to do,
weighed down by the green,
trees that cannot stir even a needle,
O trees! Trees
and the magical stillness!

As I stand, touching my forehead
in dizziness that came on
like a sudden shower,

O bird,
bird,
you are crossing
the desert of my soul.

(CP 273)

Delight

1

This delight at first
was a small flower seed
that grew to be a great joy, growing day and night.
Now it stands
uncertain, flowering tree;
and now it has become flames
that will not be blown out
by compunction's wind.

2

Awakening from early morning sleep,
my mind, moving restlessly,
is like a pair of ginko nuts,
one part sorrow, one
happiness.

I will not speak,
I will not say that word, this time,
even though I die.
That single word,
the name for my mind
on that day long ago
when the skies fell around me.

(CP 290)

Us My Child

Let us go, then, my child,
go to the sea, too.

Your long-legged daddy
is by the sea.
My precious baby,
your brilliant, sparkling black eyes;
shall I show you the sight of the sea?

Anyway, my little baby,
do you want to go to the sea?

A certain man I saw only once
and then never have seen again:
I wonder if he stands there like the sailing boat
spreading its arms against the sea wind.

Your mother is getting old
from too much searching with a careful eye
for a person
standing afar.

Am I
a blind echo
secretly that scrapes
along the bottom of the night sea?

(CP 296)

Impression of May

Oh May
even your shadows seem so bright!

To escape you,
I went to the edge of the earth where you would not be.
Yet I meet you everywhere, anywhere.
Already there, you are waiting.

Truth
becomes known as time passes.
I'll never forget you, I'll remember you for eternity,
lovely fate of mine!

I vow to myself
never again shall I wander so.

No impasse, but an opening
passage for these two
souls.

(CP 300)

Ode to Autumn Sunlight

I long for you,
and my heart,
mellowed by the autumn glow,
becomes music.

In a hushed silence
my ripened yearning
becomes the fruit,
bending the branch where it hangs.

It becomes a flock of doves
making an impatient exit
from my long-suffering heart.

Such yearning becomes a bunch of flowers
and also a field of reed flowers
that undress and rest in the wind.

With autumn sunlight
I'd dry my tears.
Though my love for you grows even stronger
in the autumn sun,
my waiting silently piles up
and turns to fallen leaves.

Ah —
I would rather be waters of the long river
lying in the evening sun's embrace.

I long for you;
my sorrowful heart
darkens into the night sky.

(CP 303)

From *Snowy Day* (1971)

Woman's Song

1

The sea is great tears.
Sobbing softly, it follows the moon.
Should
the tears vanish,
a vast plain emerges.
The sea still is tears,
and pouring out, settling, returning,
yet again vanishes.
However often,
it is because of the moon.

2

What shall I make of it, this wind?
With even the briefest touch of this chill wind upon my
    skin, hair
salty with a human smell
ten fingers reach in and grasp in a bunch,
I go mad, shuddering
with a crimson sensuality.

Never, I never knew
that the blood could run so sweet!
Ah, only if I give this flesh
entirely to the wind, to the wind,
shall I live.

3

A man of today's world

cannot sustain me
by love alone,
and yet if God allows only one thing,
I would take a man to keep.

The longing
of the national anthem,
sung in unison by a war-defeated people,
and that earnest hope
I would embrace.

(CP 316)

A Woman

I came to the plain measured by the nightfall,
and found women weeping also by the weeping tree.
The salty content, mixed with women's tears,
was carried by the wind
from the vaguely distant sea;
the salinity permeated the air with a touch of the
tradition and the impression of the mysterious
land across the sea.

Dark, empty, and maddening fire pillar
that drives a foolish woman to lose her mind over a
        foolish man
by pining for him.
The fire — kindling, kindling —
forms the sea of flames,
mingling one with another, with the unbearable spirit
of the fire and then burst.
What an example of the awesome power of the fire,
filling the whole space between earth and heaven!
What aromatic essence of whirling fire!

Like an empty boat that sails along the stream,
I have been setting out to sail
the river longer than ten thousand miles.
Standing by the riverside and witnessing
the weeping women: only they seemed similar
in all strange places.

As I came to the plain embraced by the night

I found no person to enlighten me,
no one to teach me wisdom;
instead I found the women,
picking up the silver shadow of the stars,
sitting with their heads bent down.

(CP 317)

Snowy Day

The winter tree and
wind.
Like clean laundry,
the long-haired winds
are hung upon the edge of the branches all day;
neither tree nor wind remains alone.

The wind is not alone;
no one is all alone.
I am not alone either.
Even on a day when
I stood by myself under the sky,
the sky was with me always.

Life, likewise, always
exists somewhere on the stonesteps of blessings.
Love also
remains somewhere in the pebble field
of Providence.

My heart that until now found comfort in words,
finds solutions wordlessly.
I would live with a more generous attitude.
Knowing life is such a gracious feast,
I would live such a life.

The eyes of the New Year:
ice flowers of innocence,

the tears that ascended into heaven ,
now falling to the ground
join the white snow.

(CP 319)

Love Note

        I will
        go to you.
        Even at risk of my life
        will I go.
        With hands empty
        rinsed in the dew
        I will go.
        Even blind
        I will go to you.

        In this remorse
        blue as bluest waters
        as the time accumulates
        I will go.

        I will go to you
        husband in the next world
        seeking the other half of my flesh.
        Where the spirits linger
        in strands of jet-black hair,
        calling those souls one by one
        I will go.

        I will go to you.

                                    (CP 322)

To See My Lord

Little children,
let us go far away today.
We shall walk the frozen river-way in our bare feet.
Mother will carry the cold child in her arms,
and the weary child on her back.

To a lonely place
not like this world,
to a lonely place
just like this world.
Let us go to see the true bright Holy Birth!

Mother will sing a song
never sung before,
and you shall find a joy
that sings out like a hidden love told.

For a day gone mad with the beauty of the Holy Birth,
let us go and find the place where we can go as mad
        as we please.
The billions of beams of light from the Babe
consume all light; and in our need
we are following a path to a night's rest.

Little children,
sacred bodies who emerged from the torn flesh of a
        broken wing;
little ones, who laugh aloud in the midst of
        flowing tears,
let us follow this path through the gathering dusk
to see the Child.

(CP 331)

Letter

I have never met a person as lovely as you are; nor one who made me as lonely as you did. I weep whenever I think of this.

No one gave me such honesty as you. You are the brightest mirror that reflects what is within me, and as I became familiar with your depths my eyes filled with tears. This is my beginning.

I write a letter to you every day.
As I write the first sentence, you come and read, and so I have never once sent this letter.

(CP 332)

From *Love's Cursive* (1974)

Love's Cursive

1

When a woman is without love,
she doesn't know how to
become good and hopeful.

When a woman is in love,
she dies of thirst
by the well.

2

Even to the end of the earth
even to the edge of the heavens
even to a house as far as
the world beyond,
love carries the sun in the morning;
wind in the evening.

3

Even love dies of starvation;
heart stays cold after a drink
of warm water —
The sickness grows worse, my love;
O my love, you have closed your eyes!

5

As the spring
wells up soundlessly,
as the dew forms
without sound,

just so am I
drenched, and though
the electric currents touch me
I am held by silence.

6
Person who feeds me,
atom by atom:
one single spark causes
the sunrise and sunset
burning the entire sky.

8
Words are sand,
the foam carried
to the rock by the tide.

At the horizon
words will not reach
is a person whose name
cannot be spoken.

9
Today,
love comprised my character.

No, each day
love has comprised my character.

10
Love is
customary sight,

repeated encounter,
the unification of soul and body
in the past, present, future.

11

Heart that answers heart
soul that echoes soul:
I weep just to think of these,
like a hungry
and foolish child.

13

This day so lonely
one could shout for it,
in the cold spring
that gathers
at the bottom of existence,
like complete forgiveness
a love glimmers.

15

If your soul is called,
mine too answers,
shuddering to grasp
for the first time
this alliance of two souls.

21

An uninvited woman;
I live with her.
Many days, I am that woman.
So it is,

while love is a special invitation,
the reception of conscience.

31

Do not let your blood
flow, do not
love me.
Love fills me;
the two of us must consume it.

32

The more painful, love is;
the more lonely, love is.
Piled up, the more
remain, the building stones
of divine punishment.

38

How
the two people soaked
in a fall of wet snow,
in the shared chill
kiss of such
politeness!

39

You already know
my words, and I
know already their sad resemblance
to what you would say.
Words unspoken for a lifetime,
the two of us know.

43

Loving is a precious
ability, but I lack
the strength for it.
I write a note of surrender to the air.
Today
there is no other truth.

47

Rather than deserting someone,
let me be left by someone.
When two people love,
let me be first
to love.

48

Love's half moon
in the winter sky,
half shadow, half light
frozen to a crystal.

83

Love is honest farming.
It is planting in the deepest place,
and only on the very last day
reaping.

88

Though I am an ugly clay pot
I yearn to be the brazier
that carries your coals.

I wish to bear
the precious son
I do not deserve.

(CP 345)

From *Going Together* (1980)

Snow

In heaven is it always a Sunday?
O people of heaven!

From the heaven's farthest spot
that even the plane cannot reach,
the white letter, snow falls.
Such clear glistening as cannot be made
in this world, tears that froze in their gleaming —
the snow falls.

Is it always a Sunday in heaven?
Lighting the Sunday's candle,
playing the Sunday's organ,
through the quiet dreaming mildness
snow falls.

Into the heart, remote
in what cannot be spoken,
the snow falls, scattering its fiery seeds.
Flocks of glass birds come,
their feathers beating, fluttering.

(CP 383)

Sunset

1

Behold
the injured sun
its bare flesh stabbed by the sharp sword's edge!
Shed your blood, oh sun!
Let the fresh red blood spurt, oh sun!
Do that behind the black curtain,
oh, sun, sun!
I too do the same.

2

My beloved, you fathom my heart
washing the lampshade
after filling up the lamp with oil
to meet with my unfamiliar soul.
My beloved, you know
the lamp light of the soul,
dreamlike light of the hour
when life ends its words;
you know the color
of light — the degree
of its intensity at dusky sunset,
the soul's lamp
like a dream,
dream world.

3

The sky forms a sea of tears
for the sun sinking.

The eyes of the sky blur with tears.
Befitting such loss of warmth and light,
the high tide
intimidates the sky with its terrible gravity.
Nothing can prevent it.
Ah —
tears of the sky send the flood.

(CP 384)

Morning Blessing

Morning
I go to the spring,
the sweet spring wrapped tight
in the two arms of sleep:
the sound
of dew drops stirring the air.

This day
in the first dipper I raise
pure water, the clear
water- colored gems.

Leaving the spring
I go to him.
By the pillow I place the clear water.
And each morning
as he opens his eyes, I am
not there.

O blessing!
In the morning light
more precious than unrefined gold,
each day I see in gratitude
the pure reminiscence
of his being.

(CP 386)

Alchemy

1

Life
is meeting suddenly in sequence
as parting also is meeting.
Today my life is meeting with parting,
first meeting,
without any word at all to say.

2

Without practicing even once,
all at once I was born and started to live.
Each clumsy act in the course of my life
is because I went through it without any practice.
Death also will be the same awkward moment,
anxiety as of the great mountain
that rises and rises into the blue sky.

3

What will you do?
Fire spirit, heated in the iron crucible
for ten years, forty seasons,
you are not gold.
Only the fine ash, powder of gold's bones.
Having no magic formula, I might as well
fly about too.
When some blind passion takes me,
Toryŏng, my love
neither gold nor stone,
what will you do?

(CP 388)

The Cold

I greet the cold.
I brocade and piece together
the fabric of the cold
and sleep on the cold wooden pillow
at night.
Like a couple fated to be man and wife,
the cold and I have become part of each other.
I could not have met my beloved
without the cold knowing.

Four seasons of cold.
Refreshing sound of the organ.
Though my beloved leave me
some day in middle age,
the cold is old and familiar to me.

Now as my hair is turning white,
there is no reason for me to be disturbed
by feelings left unspoken.
Today I am just an old organ
that sings a low melody.
An old musical instrument,
I subside as the heart of the cold does,
into age.

(CP 389)

Morning Prayer

Passing the long, thirsty night
and the dawn's path just before first light,
I greet the sprouting seed.
As love brings tears,
life too, and I
make my greeting to each.

Lord,
if you still have
permission left to grant me,
I would wash the feet
of someone, silently,
for a long time,
with tears, fragrant oils, and shining black hair,
as a certain woman once did for you.

This morning
this one wish
is my prayer.

(CP 396)

Hands

1

For my left hand
He gave me a right hand too.
Two hands meet after slicing the empty air;
such a pitiful sight!
Both hands of custom,
for the first time grasping the other's significance,
they hold together
like two people
just returned from travelling to the far ends of the earth.

2

Raising the void in reverence
with my two hands
makes a ceremonial table in the infinite air.
This is my all, I tell him
with my whole being.
The ceremonial wine of the refreshing wind.

3

With no one to caress,
a woman's hands
are the loneliest part of the whole body.
They are the loneliest, indeed,
of all things between heaven and earth.

4

I have come down a road lined with trees
that seemed to be within my reach,

and yet
of their leaves, just one
is left in my hand.

(CP 398)

Life

Life
comes with its cold body.
The winter barley growing stubbornly
from the naked, frozen ground,
Mother of life, even she
came with her cold body
from a distant place.

And truth, shattered,
also comes, burning in fire.
Tossed aside, bleeding,
it comes.

Behold the winter trees
that groom themselves with the razor of cold.
See the leaves that fall down and are called away
to the providence of future days,
and the branch, charged with electricity,
that turns to flint.

A person who does not know
how to love cracked or misshaped things
is not a friend.
One who cannot kiss
the scarred and injured skin
is not a friend.

Life comes with its cold body.
Passing the twelfth portal

of cold, in the large flakes
of snow falling down white,
it comes.

(CP 399)

The Setting Sun

At sunset by the East Sea,
two young brothers, soaked in the scarlet hue,
are gazing at the horizon.
Do my sons
shed tears
seeing the blood-drenched sinking sun?

When all creation
draws near in such a towering passion,
I chose to give myself to weeping.
Animate time and space;
nature's huge and perfect
respiratory system.
Inner waves, the billions, shuddering:
that love in subsiding
becomes compassion
is the truth of this woman
of forty years.
Foolishly,
again I am weeping.

(CP 402)

Mary Magdalene

When I pray,
I see a woman
who appears as a pattern of dancing sunrays
in the shadow of my Lord.

Two thousand years of time
that would surely melt any rock.
A woman with a heart in flames,
burning like a brazier for two thousand years:
with long, black hair,
a Jewess, barefoot,
she follows the Lord
constantly, everywhere.

I am no match
for this woman,
the one of sin,
repentance,
and pealing resonance.
I cannot approach
such a woman, Mary Magdalene,
with her soul seared by burns.
My spirit faint as I kneel in prayer:

Where in the sky then
will my iniquities, my repentance, my lamentations
find haven of rest?

(CP 403)

Wind

The wind is blowing.
Where the wind blows
to the end of the world
I would follow.

Sunlight:
you nourish
the soft-skinned fruit,
but it is the wind that whispers
round the borders of the orchard,
almost but not quite the lonely
whistler.

Those without a place
to hold them in this life
may have been the winds
of a previous life.
Wearing coat and hat, the winds
may have come to visit.

Fond of the wind, I would go
as the winds go.
They go together,
and though they part,
one goes ahead and waits.
That is what I like
best in the winds.

When the wind blows

I would go with it.
Where it goes, far and far away
I would be its bride.

(CP 412)

Spring

Today the green color of new birth sprouts like the
1919 March First Hurrahs! shouted everywhere
throughout the nation.

Nevertheless, how much more moving to witness their
rising from winter's roots. Even under the soil, dark and
ice-locked, they have endured, maintaining their straight
posture like bronze nails. For all its tears, life's sun-
seeking faith.

The one who keeps most to silence, knows best how to
see the preparation for life; because of the bruises, the
season is all the more painfully splendid — young as
young and undefiled spring!

(CP 413)

*March 1, 1919: The Korean independence demonstrations
against Japanese colonial occupation.*

Candle Light

1

Candle,
neither in one of my love songs
nor in the love itself that passes beyond
that song, climbing the folds of mountain ridges,
nor in the completeness of my life
shall you
who burns without ash
be surpassed.

2

Brightly, so bright
the one
passing my soul
making me weep,
whose vermilion skirt's edge
even the wind does not stir.

3

All living things
watch in dread
this person, the one
burning in her own oil.
God Himself
for a moment pauses
in His work.
Utterly consumed,
in parting this world
you drive the nail
into a black coffin.

4
O Brightness
stronger than despair!
Magnetism
of existence that does not expire
even as it burns,
O love!

5
Candle light,
with music
warming the hands until dusk

Ah, suddenly in the attire
of sunset
brimming,
you are the very one
whose figure stayed in my thoughts
three hundred years or more.

6
Bit of wax
touching flame becomes oil,
turning clear becomes distilled water,
again congealing
becomes oil, becomes wax
until its discarded
body turns again

to flame

7

A lonely lad
of long ago
and a girl
grew up accustomed to their loneliness
serving in order
their long, lonely time
until they met
one later day.
We light
one candle in consecration.
Lord God the Creator,
grant us the blessing of age.

8

Not even once
to have known
a woman,
this fresh
inexperience,
wick
of chastity!

9

There is no one
who rode down in a gold bucket
the thousand, ten thousand
fathoms in the water.
At the bottom in cold, cold water
there is no one

who found the blind
and freezing woman
but you.

10
Just washed,
rinsed clear,
my soul
removes its clothing
and enters alone
into a room
filled with the candle-lit body.

11
The candle knows
the wisdom that loving
purifies sin.
And human destiny
joining sin and love,
blood and flesh
the candle knows
the pity of it.

12
Winter trees,
candles grown life-size.
Fresh-blooded
phosphorescence
presses its kiss
on the flesh
of abstinence.

13
Having risen
into heaven,
have the candles become
stars?
And do the stars
all night
let fall their rain
of light?

14
Look at me,
look at the woman
who is done with words of love.
Look
at the candle
so truly pitiful
that shrivels
away in her hand.

15
Cutting off the flame
with the razor's blade
I cry.
My tears
endlessly fall at the sight
of the severed tongues
of flame
joining again.

16

Not such a light
as illuminates the body,
nor yet the light
of the heart,
I would be
the shadow of the light
of the room
next to your soul.

17

Forgive
forgive me.
Hear my entreaty,
far darker wish
ten fingers burnt
offering, kindling
the fire offering,
please accept me.

18

For a thousand days, the one
I longed to see who for a thousand
days did not come, when the faint light
touches the paper of the door,
the candle light's rough illumination,
even after many more thousands
of days I
would open the door.

19

Devoted to heaven
together with you

— granted from heaven
together with you
— this
is my prayer.

20
Singing
a song of flame and light,
flying the kite of fire
and light
candles, the pure
unwordly
children.

21
Go to sleep, just
go to sleep
eyelid sleepless through an entire life.
Like love
exhausted,
ah, in death at last
closing its eye
— the candle's light.

22
You shall not weep alone
you shall not sleep
alone, out in the open
your candle drops
all turn to flame,
my body, transparent
will embrace you

even after I die.

23

After all is done
you who rose
in smoke that could not express
whatever might have been said,
in the empty bowl that was given nothing,
you cast the shadow
of another life's
sun.

24

Soul of two
standing open,
be like the candle's light:
May we learn only
silence
and the burning.

25

The candles of the world
make a unified
religion
of long ago
and today:
turning to heaven
and burning,
return to heaven.

(CP 420)

From *Light and Silence* (1983)

Love Song

From deepest root
to topmost crown
my loneliness
is what I must give
to you.
This heart
circling the seamless ring
of heaven from origin in the east
past the end of the western horizon
returns once again.

(CP 433)

Song of the *Pip'a**

If it is not quiet
the song of this *pip'a* cannot be heard.
If the wind does not sleep
the light of this oil lamp
will die out.

A person of former times
giving a sign of being near,
bathes,
combs the hair
and plays this melody,
lighting the candle
for the prayers of former times.

In youth my love
was a chain of rose thorns.
Now my love
I place before my beloved's feet
as shoes freely given.

The song of the *pip'a*,
O song of the *pip'a*!

My burning heart
burns completely and knows peace.
Comprehended for the first time,
the *pip'a's* song causes tears.

(CP 435)

* 4-stringed traditional musical instrument

The Sea

O sea,
after you had borne
my loved one
to the horizon and beyond,
every day
I set one peach from heaven
on the table.

My ceremony
of remembering,
for a thousand days
loosing my hair
for the vast expanse of the sea.
Before I knew,
the hair by my ear
turned frost white.

What shall I do?
What shall I do?

Today
the branch of heaven's peach
bends toward the sea in my soul.

(CP 436)

Longing

Some day I would ask

whether happy or sad,
on sick days or well,
dreaming or awake,
thoughts of you
make the wires of my soul
whine — such a fierce intensity!
How strange — this echo that others cannot hear:
your voice
crosses through my bones
every season, all my life.
Before I die,
someday I would ask just once
if you felt the same as I.

(CP 437)

Having Come To The Mountain

In the rain, Mount Sŏrak
wears the cloud band on its forehead
and fog below its bosom.
Those who know one another
beyond words, touched
in the flesh
as in a hazy dream.

Trees
and rocks
are without names,
like the unknown soldiers
or the early saints
who lost their names.

Living on the green mountain,
those who have forgotten their own names,
just as their bodies stand naked in the rain
are at peace
and warm.

Today I have learned the reason,
why a person who has died
comes to be held in the mountain's embrace.

(CP 438)

Gift

1

I am earth,
yet you light me
like a candle.
All of my life
I have been a stone,
and yet you pattern me
like a jade.
For the first time,
I experience
such a miracle in my life.

2

Loving more, the more I can love,
and praying, the more I can pray...
Such a strange swelling;
a strange power, not at all
my own.

3

What you gave,
the leaves
and flowers,
yield to fruit
as time passes.
Today,
I receive
a golden seed
that passed through the scorching heat
of the sun.

(CP 439)

Night Letter

Let me write a letter.

Finished with the day's talk,
after practicing alone
without a lapse, old as I am
let me write the letter
late at night, one phrase
each day.

The sense of death
with the dew that falls
at evening prayer,
of the melody played low
by candle light,
may they wet the winter pillow.
With my heart tightened in pain,
let me love the nights
that die in bearing the dawn.

As time passes,
my fervor for life becomes
vivid, actual.
When I was young, my heart
spoke out.
Now, at this stage of my life,
I shall record
as my unalterable will
what has pierced me
to the marrow.

Let me record also
that to love each day
is also to die each day.

Let me also put down freely
the night wanderings of a soul
carried back from the ends of the earth
on the currents of a windy day
like a snowflake tossed in a storm.

Then on the night
when my letter has reached an end,
let the light of a distant star
be the period.

(CP 441)

Fall

Touched by the flame
of a single match,
untying their skirts
and tossing them away,
again and again, these
autumn woods.

(CP 443)

Happiness

A bird and I,
a winter tree and I,
heavy snow at dusk and I,
if I love a bird, will it be happy?
If I love a tree, will it be happy?
If I love a snowflake, will it be happy?

A bird loves a bird
a tree loves a tree
if a brother and sister of a snowflake love each other,
they would be surely happy.

As these things in nature,
if you and I loved each other,
keeping our grieving hearts deep inside ourselves,
we might hear the sudden tune of an organ played by
    God;
we might have jeweled ears then.

(CP 443)

Love's Words

1
Love
is unspoken words.
Unbearably bright love
like the morning sun awakening us from our
    sound sleep,
builds a home within the lipless soul
and lives hidden
behind a folding screen in the farthest room
reached after
passing through the front and middle
gates of the house.

Like an ancient Eastern crescent moon,
and the stars, decorated with golden threads,
love buried so deep in thought,
never utters a single word.

2
For speaking of love
heaven and earth were set on fire,
and as the punishment demanded,
he and I were parted.
As my life
grew quite dark,
I met him again
to say farewell.
Ah, even after pouring out so many thousands of times,
the evening sky so crimson.

And love
even in the mistake of speaking it
is beautiful.

(CP 445)

Hymn

He has returned.
He has entered by the twig gate
of his old home.
This fact alone
lights the candle above my pillow
each night.

I will not speak.
I will not say anything.
The candle as it consumes its own body
is also silent.

My heart grows warm,
and my soul weeps
at the dew-washed beauty
of the world at night.
All is peaceful
beneath the undeserved shower
of star light.

He has returned.

(CP 449)

The West

Whatever you might
do, what of that?

Like the shadow lying on the ground
or the wind falling upon the shadow
and the black river flowing above the wind:
what if it is night, what of that?

And what if it is not visible?
If the sea bottom is dug deeper
and the waters rise another stage,
and in the sky above the heavens
a flock of geese fly away with their honking, honking,
or if at times their flight
is not seen, what of that?

What of separation?
Or if the sun and moon go their separate ways?
What if they do not meet?
If each
sinks into the west,
the west.

(CP 450)

The Winter Tree

Will you tell the story?
Are you going to?
That no one came all winter;
will you start the story there?
Will you echo such a tale,
O my tree of winter?

The white wind
that passes by
might be the pleated skirts of the snow woman
or the white locks of that woman who has lived
longer than the mountain god ...
Will you tell this kind of story?
Will you echo yet again
the tale?

Music that cleanses my soul
and makes me weep heedlessly
— will you let me hear it?
Will you let me hear
the aftertone, desolate nature's
echo that makes the nine heavens
resonate —

Will you let me
hear it, O my winter tree?

(CP 451)

Winter Christ

Today
as he walks the snow-covered hills and fields
his clothes are white as the snow,
and his bare feet are whiter still.

Where long ago he crossed over the waters,
the river now is frozen,
a vast crystal of ice.
He crosses over
the piercing, needle-sharp cold.
His bare feet, whiter than white.

I would weep.
Lord of the snowy day
ceaselessly, ceaselessly
drawing the blood of the new spring
mixed with his precious blood
from all the depths of earth
and sea in this fathomless,
hair-raising cold.

(CP 452)

New Year

As I look back,
summer was fiery and dry,
yet failed to heat the blood of a man.
Autumn taught me an inner thought,
but I did not much care.

A year's worth of sun and shade
has poured out.
From beyond the wholly empty sky,
like a dream
the snow falls and scatters.

Truly a blessing,
a healing in whiteness.
As I light the candle,
all under heaven becomes an altar.
Fearsome and too great an honor for me
is that life.

(CP 454)

Response

So still,
dewdrop forming
on the young grasses and trees,
and sunlight
that arrays all things in the universe
with fragrant oil.
Fog and haze,
or wind that gently unties the roll of silk,
a single word be without.

Being so still,
without a sound of thunder
the heart opens its door
and builds a path to visit by
between two souls.

Truly, for each birth
one who has prepared the far-off-day's
name and blessing,
pours the living water's infinite
sweetness, even in the moment of trial,
harmony most precious.

Still.
The resounding sequence
passes by,
and there remains
only the most ardent stillness,
meaning and the reply.

(CP 456)

To Spring

1

Accompanying no one
bringing nothing,
spring, each year
you arrive all alone and then
leave with empty hands.
Reflecting on this fifty years after my birth,
I find you, spring, splendidly handsome.
With your naked hands, feet, and frizzy hair —
the only signs of your beauty —
you are gorgeous, spring.

2

Even our brief meeting
has left me quenched
after a few years of thirst.
My life-thirst is quenched
from our meeting.
Here, where sunlight
drenched this spot, you and I met,
then drifted apart.
The single thirst left to me now
is for my journey to the next world.
Spring! I am circled
by the most dream-like sunlight
of this present world.

(CP 458)

Poet

1

Cutting the crystal
carefully, as I
gradually become afraid
of this work.

3

Poets genuine
as true jade
— this thirst
of our age
More
depth and more
height and more
breadth
The first sprouting of the grass
in that nakedness, that stillness —
suddenly
you my love
shall see.

(CP 467)

Departure

I would travel to find a new friend
who will shower love on me.
I would find the young shepherd boy
who was passing by, playing
a reed flute.
Just after the pompous parade of the honorable person,
I would meet the shepherd boy,
whose stage
of youthful manhood was as lonely
as my youngest son's;
whose dreams and hopes
were not realistic, yet pure
and lofty.

With my life's love still left within me,
so it would not turn to heartache.
I would prepare myself
in a careful way
and take a journey
to a far distant place,
to the end of life
I would go.

I will be content
after emptying all the love
that has been left within me.

(CP 480)

Day's End

As the day darkens, my love
too grows dark.

Soul of one alone
since the first day:
love as well
is being alone,
like the candle consuming
its own body
as it dreams of burning forever;
the wax, soon little, then less,
the light dying away,
like the candle
leaving not even ash.

As the day darkens, love as well
grows dark, and life,
and the thought of seeing you
day or night, the four seasons through,
that too drains away bit by bit.
With the times
and the love of a person
alone on the last day,
the soul too being alone,
closing its eyes
in the embrace of the Supreme Being.

(CP 483)

From *Christening Of The Wind* (1988)

To Winter

Come on in
winter,
I unfasten a door for you.

This year's unusual cold
that chilled my hands and feet
even in the midst of sultry summer:
that summer and autumn came and now have
        gone away.
Just in your proper turn,
You came running,
winter,
so do come in.

You must have brought
the ice-woven cushion
rolled up from your place
of iceberg habitation
at the North Pole.
Set it down,
winter.

Frozen wound
that cannot weep,
burning dagger scar.
And yet, how clean
and transparent,
such a crystal knife!

Your cold heart
is still honest, it tells
no lies.
And for the revival of spring,
you sprinkle your water
as if pouring onto the bean sprouting sieve.

Whatever is to follow,
first come in,
winter.

(CW 20)

Grassland

People hoping to learn how you are
study the expression
in my eyes,
and doing so
they may have glimpsed the grassy field,
the deep green of the grasses
that would be turned up
at the edge of the lamp's light,
no matter how deep the winter
and the snow.
Even late at night,
they would have seen
the sleepless grassy field
covering you,
a bolt of cotton
of the deepest green blood.

(CW 36)

Summer Tree

August tree
spends the night of love
before the day of parting.
Within the tree
feeding separately each other —
the faithful love of branches
leaves and roots —
the ripened fruit is taken,
the leaves wither.

O August tree!
You put on the color of darkest green
and the fragrant, coral-hued oils.
O beauty of the branches
that in their affection bless and caress each other freely.

Shameful, the people
through insufficient love, hasty parting,
who wall up their hearts
even as time still remains.

O nature
forgive those among humankind who have gone away,
as those among us still
who sent them.

(CW 68)

This Summer

I'd lose God this summer
someone had prophesied.
Even before the advent of summer
my God had already left
and secluded Himself in a remote, secret site.

What event then
might occur to me?
Would all the flourishing achievements of the past
wither away after losing their splendor?
With only the tear-soaked bread to give me strength,
I wonder if I could lift up
the weight of my mundane life;
I wonder if I could erect
a virtuous wall of hope.

I embraced all things around me with all my heart
when I was in love.
With such pure and immaculate gratitude,
I wish to set a table
and dedicate it to the One
Whose hands and feet were nailed.
I wish to return my debt to the One,
the source of all gifts.

Kneel, kneel down!
After the sprout of a repentant soul has started,
and make a wild grassfield

where the wind whispers,
that He surely will visit and harvest.
I would then rise up,
and all those who had been kneeling
would rise up together.

Summer that has lost faith,
that closed its eyes
upon the grief-stricken stone,
I know one thing at least:
that this is not all.

(CW 70)

Trees III

So still!
Knowing not how to leave,
nor yet how to come near,
O trees,
Where you rise up
you shake off all your leaves;
you bathe
in the cold of heaven's waterfall.
You make
no other sound
than the blood running beneath
the cold, numb flesh
of your naked body.

Even though you do gaze
at one another,
this is not
something that will cause a sound.

(CW 72)

Your Life

Your
shabby childhood;
boyhood in a time of war.
Young manhood carrying stones on your back.
Long adulthood when fire and ice
clasp hands in turn
in punishment.
Nearing the edge of the cliff,
today's weather is normal,
and your old age has already begun.

It is all right
now; it is all right, all right.
Isn't there a woman
bending her back to bow
to all those years
of your life?

(CW 90)

A Fine Day

Today is a fine day.
The sun is up and the wind is blowing.
It is a very pleasant day.
I don't have even a headache.
Sorrows grew up
then moved away from me.
After passing all my youthful years,
I became attached to this way of life.
What a wonderful day it is!

A happy day,
I prayed for thousands of days of my life
that a happy day would come.
As I climbed a mountain and pointed to a distant place,
I found myself greeting a visitor in a cotton garment,
one who wore reading glasses,
and had left his silk gown and hat elsewhere.
If I ever fall in love again
at my fairly old age,
a fairly old person
may well be suitable.

Upon a tree,
where the leaves are aflame with autumn hues,
the clouds rest.
The fabric of an impartial sky
covers all things in the universe
with its single sheet.

So it shall be.
So it shall be.
So it shall be.

(CW 91)

Your House

I will build a house for you,
my beloved,
in a secret place that no one can find,
I will prepare a haven of rest in this world
with doors facing the east, west, south, and north;
a house with all doors open to the four seasons.

When the world takes its hands off
at the end of your life-long journey,
leaving you all alone,
would you, my beloved, come to me
without leaving a trace of your finger prints
on the side posts of the door?
The sensation of thirst at midnight;
your incurable habit:
Ah, would you, my beloved, come
and fill where I am empty?

A place no one dares to inhabit,
where only the wind dwells in comfort
at a time when no one seems to visit,
will you come and stay in your place?
Then my sky would become a moonlight evening.

I will build a house for you,
my beloved.
Like unfastening the tie of a blouse,
untie the string of deep injuries from worldly affairs,
and the bruises of yesterdays are erased.

Take rest, find refuge.
Just casting a glance at you
causes me to weep.
I would become huge arms for you,
become like a high fence around you.

(CW 96)

Prayer For New Year's Morning

Grant us to gaze at the snow falling on the
    green mountain
at first glimpse upon our awakening.
Grant us to hear the sound of the green wind,
brushing through the pine trees
whose roots have spread under the rocks.
Grant us the inheritance of a shower of blessings
you prepared and then cultivated
since the Genesis.
Grant us to carry
the cornerstone of mission
as front runner, girded with a vital, young heart,
in this era.

Grant us the ability
to discern a true friend from the first meeting.
And grant us to anoint and embrace
the inner person in each.
In the depths of our soul,
the life of life,
grant us such an orchard, covered with fruit trees of
    all seasons.
Grant us to offer you, my Lord,
the sweetest fruit
for your meal
each day.

(CW 108)

New Poems

To the Spring Again

Oh spring of the year!
Having no role, I will leave
your stage.
This too, Oh spring!
I know
you have taken another lover.

How clumsy! How naive,
the warm heart alone
is unfamiliar with the ways
of side-long glances:
left behind like the scars
of whips on the slaves of old,
Oh Spring of this year!
Cold the wind and snow
that come to spread their bitter taste
on your budding:
I would meet them halfway.
I would carry them
away on my own back

Grass

and so it
comes to be here

Long days' coldness
through the green scratched in the soil
even before
grass seed carried in winds
yet higher
more green
and higher
more green
who has commanded?

Open the eyes
unlock the mind
Open the eyes
inlock the mind,
Did someone whistle it?

The vivid dye
dressed in fold upon fold
of dark, dark green,
becoming the single tuft, here,
of grass, all through the hot spell,
and here, through the hot nights
the new seed of grass forming
the strong life root
strikes deeper,
just now
sufficient to become
the grass.

The Making and Being Made

A needle pierces the cloth,
the cloth feels the pain of the piercing
but in the end a suit of clothes is made:
so, in Kang Chŏngjung's "Song of the Needle."

Threaded needle repeatedly
penetrating the cloth;
heated iron passing over and over:
from such extreme misery
are clothes surely made.

At the sharp scissoring
every entryway cut off,
pieces of scrap cloth
that will not meet the needle and iron
are even more disappointing.

Ring of carved jade,
flesh-furrowing fife;
even the apple that has been peeled for the feast
the cold brutality
of the making and the being made
makes me shudder
as I am pierced by its needle.

Renunciation

Seen from the skies,
the ground is a deep
and distant ending,
as far below the translucent depth
of their acquiescent descent
through air like freezing cold water,
the white snow,
sisters lying down in order:
such utter stillness.
Reaching the end,
without a trace of wind
renunciation
of the one resting.

Of all these
mine only is the dark body.
Frozen crisp under the snow,
the dark plain:
I am the offspring
of what is called the soil.
Yet I too
close my eyes
today in the arms of renunciation.

Afterword

Notes on Kim Namjo's *Collected Poems*
by Kim Yunsik, Seoul National University

With only a modest amount of attention given, anyone can be pleased with a poem, and what is more, seem to find some consolation in it. Is this because writing poetry is the most blameless of all human activities? So to participate in a poem, to wander around in it, is blameless as well? Yet when it comes to analyzing a poem, no one seems to have any confidence. A poem is something like a bell situated out of doors in a place with no roof, the sound muffled by falling snow. Trying to explain or interpret such a phenomenon is impossible; or rather, explanation and interpretation are like the foggy trace of the breath which makes the sound of the bell seem impure.

Because a poem's echo is so slight, the changes it makes in us are subconscious ones. But a poem is inevitably made of words, that most dangerous of all our human possessions. That truth is inescapable. And while it may be true that beauty makes us quite silent, the only way to avoid the difficulties of interpreting poetry is to decrease the number of times we discuss it. What does this mean? There seem to be two ways to accomplish this. One is to own the poem. Suppose we see a painting in the museum. In this case, to own the painting is to possess the visitor's gaze, the position, color, and smell of the painting. This is also true in the case of a poem. It is to possess the book of a certain size, but also the paper of a certain quality, the shape of the printed characters, the book's appearance in the store where it was sold, and even the photograph of the poet, the clothing, the voice, the style of walking, the hand writing.

The other approach is to create a space or circumstance in which beauty can be placed. Beauty is not something that can be situated anywhere, and just as ideal states of the world are suitable to specific

137

eras, art also comes to occupy a specific position for its image. The position is like that of a king, not because of any love for noble emotion or nobility, but simply because it can express freedom of will and creativity. I shall try this latter approach.

From her best known poem, and her most persistent theme, everyone in Korea knows the poet Kim Namjo as a poet of the candle, and of love. Thus we have to examine the relationship between a candle and love in order to understand her. It is love that we really want to know. What is love, that has no shape or scent in the physical world? Who can reveal it? Human beings have always been trying to know the reality, but it cannot be shown to us at all. Love is not only a great subject, but also a desire profound as the ocean. The fact that Kim Namjo has a mission to show to us the reality of love itself, or to look for it by herself through her entire life, reveals her true poetic passion and aesthetic desire.

The essential point cannot be found only in the pairing of passion and intention; the key point is in what she creates. Certainly the use of the extended trope of the candle is part of Kim Namjo's artistic triumph. She was not the first to write of the candle, but no one has pursued it as thoroughly and continuously as she. This is the result of her serious and eager inquiry as to the nature of love. To analyze the seriousness and eagerness, it is necessary to explore the method of its expression. And for the expression of love, the mysterious human character of the candle, we need to begin with the assumption that we do not know its reality. We can know it only by analogy. This analogy is developed in two images: one, the complete burning of itself, and the other, the burning for itself. The mission of versification is to reveal the shapeless and functioning love in the real world, through the images of the poem. We can see, hear and touch it in the images of love drawn by analogy to the aspects of the candle.

The creation of the image is concealed in the candle. Just as fire and light are unified in the candle, love turns out to be one through the poem. How could the red fruit be born without the progress of the burning, of itself and entirely for itself? And yet it cannot be said that the reality of love has been revealed; only the edge of its robe has been glimpsed.

What I have been describing up to this point is really quite useless as an explanation of the poetry. It is no more than a way to fashion a little room in which Kim Namjo's poems may by placed. But if something more is permitted, I would be willing to add the following. In this collection, there are two poems from which the most intensive glances seem to come directly at me: "Alchemy", and "Grassland". They are where the world, love, the soul dare not intrude, and they occupy a territory in which love and soul can have no resolution

> What will you do?
> Fire spirit, heated in the iron crucible
> for ten years, forty seasons,
> you are not gold.
> Only the fine ash, powder of gold's bones.
> Having no magic formula, I might as well
> fly about too.
> When some blind passion takes me,
> Toryŏng, my love
> neither gold nor stone,
> what will you do?

This poem possesses the formality of Kim Namjo's other poems but also the severity needed to go beyond the formality. To this poet, love may mean a thing of the earth; and after passing through the alchemy of the severe attitude, it becomes possible at last to reach the light of "Grassland".

> People hoping to know how you are
> study the expression

in my eyes,
and doing so
they may have glimpsed the grassy field,
the deep green of the grasses
that would be turned up
at the edge of the lamp's light,
no matter how deep the winter
and the snow.
Even late at night,
they would have seen
the sleepless grassy field covering you,
a bolt of cotton
of the deepest green blood.

Here is the look of eyes that only those can possess who have burned all of themselves, and burned for themselves. No one can say that this mature scene, created in reality of love, is not the realization of a true poetics.

CORNELL EAST ASIA SERIES

For ordering information, please contact:
Cornell East Asia Series
East Asia Program
Cornell University
140 Uris Hall
Ithaca, NY 14853-7601
USA
(607) 255-6222.

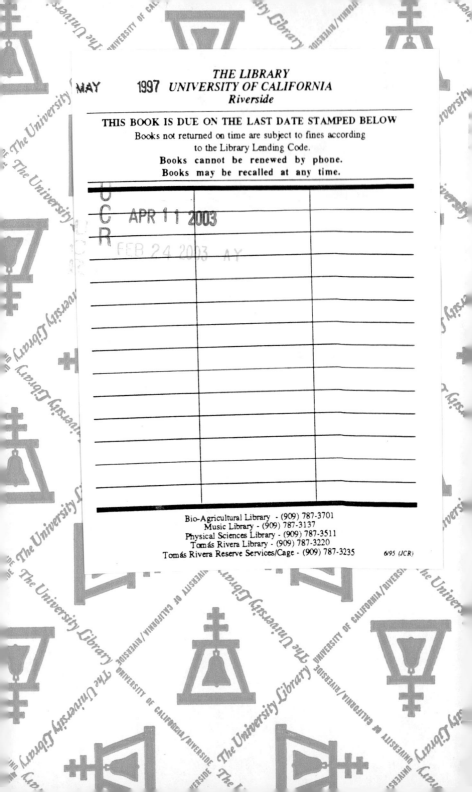